FELLOWSHIP
OF THE
POTS

FELLOWSHIP
OF THE
POTS

A True Account of Divine Design

CATHY HARTLEY

5 TWO
PRESS

Thank you, Jesus and John.
Jesus, for rescuing me so long ago and daily since then.
John, for walking with me for more
years than seems possible.

CONTENTS

Clay doesn't talk back to the fingers that mold it, saying, "Why did you shape me like this?" Isn't it obvious that a potter has a perfect right to shape one lump of clay into a vase for holding flowers and another into a pot for cooking beans?

—Romans 9:20-21 (The Message: The Bible in Contemporary Language)

CHAPTER 1

FABULOUSLY AVERAGE

I am not funny, smart, or pretty. Well, wait. I am funny enough, even though my husband tells me that I am not funny. Humorous, maybe, but not funny. I am smart enough when compared with the totally uneducated, and I am barely pretty enough—in the right light with hair and makeup just so. Except for the aforementioned, I am average in every sense of the word—height, weight (OK, above average here), income, and social status. Average, normal, typical, run-of-the-mill, common, ordinary. Therein lies the rub. I do not want to be average. No one celebrates average. I want to be fabulous and glorious and noticed and celebrated! Yes! That's it! I would like to be celebrated. Don't you? I want people to applaud and cheer when I enter a room. I want my name to be whispered in awe in public settings. I want to be considered wonderfully worthwhile. Is that too much to ask? It seems that it is. We do not celebrate average. We celebrate pretty and brave and wealthy and funny and famous. We celebrate celebrities who are celebrities for no other reason than that they are celebrities! Oh, we celebrate, but no one celebrates average.

Since most of us want to be celebrated, we compare, we control, and we cover. We compare ourselves with others. If we compare often enough, trust me, we *will* discover someone to whom we feel superior. We white-knuckle control the very breath out of ourselves and others, leaving little room for creativity and freedom. We cover the truth of our ordinariness with a blanket knitted of the need to be significant.

Imagine for a minute a world in which average is fabulous. A world in which we do not have to try so hard to win and to succeed and to pretend to be someone that we are not. Imagine celebrating each other just for being, well, average. And we are all average—most of the time. Wait, what? I can hear some of you now: "We cannot possibly celebrate average! It's positively un-American! If we celebrate average, what exactly is our motivation to be better, to do better, to have more?" Thoughts that scream "You *must* be, do, have more!" saturate our minds. We teach our children that they absolutely must succeed and that to succeed, they must *exceed* others. There can be no place for average. More, more, more. Too much pressure.

I want to suggest that, just for a moment, we opt out of the "we *must* be, do, have more" pressure cooker and allow ourselves time and space to be simply us. In that space, we just might find peace and freedom and, more important, the Divine.

Every person is delightfully created and crafted as a vessel for the Divine. Think about that. You, me, everyone—holders of the sacred, the eternal, the holy. The challenge is that our average humanness mixes with the sacred divine and that makes each of us holy to a greater or lesser degree. I am going to define *holy* as "set apart for divine use," and the degree to which we allow that divine use dictates our degree of holiness. Do we dare to believe, *really believe*, that we, in all our averageness, are carriers of God-presence? Could that belief take us out of the realm of average and into the realm of divine? Can it possibly be that you and I are designed for a greater purpose just by virtue of our existence? Not because we are perfect, or even close to perfect, but because there is a creative God whose plan is to lovingly allow every one of us to live an over-the-top life of fulfilled dreams.

The access to that plan is Jesus. He is the road to God's plan, the source of all that is true, and the absolute fullness of life. When I was much younger, I used to hear people say, "Jesus is the answer." I could not help but wonder how they knew that Jesus was the answer if they did not know what the question was. As I have grown in years and, hopefully, wisdom, I have come to understand that it does not matter what the question is, Jesus *is* the answer. Are you sick, depressed, and in danger of losing hope that things can ever be different? Jesus is the answer. Out of time, energy, or money? Jesus. Do you fear that your life will never make any lasting positive impact? Again, Jesus. Do you suspect that life consists of only the daily ho-hum-do-it-again-ness and then it's over? Dare to believe that God's plan, through Jesus, will relieve your fears, flaws, and failures and guide you to the Divine.

Raise your hand if you have ever thought that life was leading you in a certain direction and, lo and behold, things took a hard left and you ended up in a completely different space than expected. Go ahead! Raise your hand! Well, that is my story.

Some years ago I had the pleasure of praying on a very regular basis with two girlfriends. Our top-secret prayer goal was that God would grab our husbands by the nape of their necks and somehow magically force them to be the men that we thought they should be. It was not long until we discovered that before we could pray for them, we had to pray for us. So our focus changed, and as our focus changed, we changed. We prayed, cried, confessed, laughed, and spent life-altering time with God. We very often prayed that God would make us vessels to be filled with divine presence, fit for His use, whatever He had planned for us. We even prayed that He would break us of our selfishness and pride so that we could be divinely used.

I have made it my business to hear and recognize God's voice. During our time together, I clearly heard Him reveal that each of us was an incredibly unique vessel. We were amazed to discover that, in our little fellowship of three, one of us was a cut crystal vase, one was a raku pot, and one a brightly colored teapot. A trio of beautiful and distinct containers. And each of us, because we chose to live a life of divine purpose and destiny, was required to experience her own, sometimes difficult, lessons intended to refine the ugly and reveal her beauty. I invite you to join me for the story of the fellowship of the pots, and, maybe, along the way you will discover what kind of vessel you are divinely created to be.

Faith is the strength by which a shattered world shall emerge into the light.

—Helen Keller

CHAPTER 2

CUT CRYSTAL VASE

Patient, painstaking precision. That is what it takes to produce a fine crystal work of art. It is only after molten glass is shaped, cooled, trimmed, and smoothed that it is given to the master glass cutter to carve into the final beauty. With steady hands and incredibly sharp tools, the artist slices exact cuts in exact spots to enhance the brilliance of each piece. One of the easiest ways to tell true crystal is to simply let light shine through it. Science geeks (and I use this phrase with utmost respect) will know that light bends when it moves through different materials. This phenomenon is called *refraction*. True crystal contains at least 24 percent lead, and that lead produces a refractive quality that casts light in different colors and different patterns, causing it to sparkle.

Combine just the right amount of material composition with precise cuts and, voilà! A work of art.

My sister-friend who is the cut crystal vase is tall and thin and naturally very lovely. You know the type— doesn't need or wear makeup and is still pretty (which is fine, if you like that sort of thing). A cut crystal vase is naturally very pretty, but the full beauty of the piece is seen only when light shines through it. We have all known naturally beautiful women whose inner being caused us to walk away thinking, "Man, she is ugly," the kind of ugly that no amount of good lighting can enhance and no amount of makeup can cover.

Then there are those women who might not have what our culture would call "natural beauty," but there is just something about them, something bright, something lit from within. We leave them feeling lighter, encouraged, and somehow better for having been with them. When God's light shines through a woman, she is beautiful. I don't care what she looks like physically.

Rufus Jones, a Quaker who lived in the late nineteenth and early twentieth century, was once speaking of the importance of having a "bright appearance." After his speech, a "plain" woman came up and asked him what he would do if he had a face like hers. He replied, "While I have troubles of my own of that kind, I've discovered that if you light it up from within, any old face you have is good enough."

Now, let me be truly clear here. I am not anti-makeup/

hair dye/cosmetic surgery. There are simply times when a girl's gotta do what a girl's gotta do. But what if we could move away from the desperate need to look a certain society-dictated way and focus more on the good stuff going on inside us? In 2019 the revenue of the cosmetic industry in the United States was well over $49 billion! That's 49 . . . billion . . . dollars! What kind of changes could we make in childhood hunger or homelessness if we stepped away from our makeup brushes for just a moment? What if we shifted our focus to growing in wisdom and goodness and graciousness and caring about other people more than what we see in the mirror? What if we began to celebrate the value of the mothers and the teachers and the caregivers more than the comparative insignificance of just being a celebrity? What if we began to look for the divine in each other, or as an old preacher once said, "Fellowship the spirit and not the flesh"? That movement would create utter upheaval! Ladies, God's light gives us the power to transform culture, and as I look, my culture could use a little transformation.

My cut crystal vase friend has both natural physical beauty and the light of God's love and presence shining fiercely through her life. Life has not always been easy for her, but she has learned to trust the Master Creator to make just the right cuts in just the right places to fashion her into an exquisite vessel.

The cuts of life can bring either beauty or destruction. You know the cuts—those life experiences accompanied by such severe soul pain that you wonder if you will even survive. Most of us have known the heartbreaking death of someone near and dear, the emptiness of a marriage divided, the overwhelming fear of incurable disease. I clearly remember trying desperately to catch my breath as the memory of an agonizing childhood cut threatened. Have you ever had the scary thought that you just may drown from emotional pain? Those are the wounds that drive so deep that you are forever changed, never to return to your earlier self. Now and then, we just shove the pain in any direction to get it away from us, even trying to forget it and go on as if nothing happened. But something did happen. Our soul was cut.

Band-Aids of food, work, drugs, drink, or sex may work for a time, but the only way to heal those cuts is to trust the Divine Glass Maker to rescue beauty from them. He will bring healing. He is sometimes called the Master Physician, and accessing His healing is much the same as visiting the doctor. First, you must recognize that you have a problem. If you have a cut, you make an appointment to see the doctor. Immediately after making this appointment, you begin to feel better, and you think that maybe you should cancel said appointment. You can probably put some antibacterial ointment on it and bandage it up yourself. "I've got this. No need to bother the doctor. And what about that co-pay? That money could be better used somewhere else. Yup. I've got this." Right up until you realize that this cut has become infected and is only getting worse. You don't got this. "OK, OK! I will see the doctor."

At the visit, you realize that this doctor is kind and seems competent. You decide that you will trust the doctor, and after your consultation, you are given meds and instructed on how to care for the wound. Rational people will follow these instructions, and most will see healing. Sometimes a follow-up visit is required for reevaluation and more help if needed. Along the way, you just may decide that it would be smart to develop a relationship with this trusted doctor in order to secure ongoing health for yourself.

Engaging the Master Physician is the same process, except there is no co-pay. Deep soul wounds can be healed only by the one who created that soul. Look at your wound just long enough to recognize that you cannot heal yourself. You need help. Let me caution against continuing to stare at the wound. Many of us get stuck right there. We cannot seem to take our focus from the fact that we have been cut and it hurts! Badly! Stop staring at the problem, and consult with the one who can help. This is called prayer. Doctor consultations require a couple of actions: You explain the problem, and then the doctor tells you the solution. The process is the same with God: You speak, then you listen. Again, this is prayer. This listening requires that we get quiet enough to hear. No small task considering our noisy lives, but totally doable. It just takes time and practice.

We must get quiet because God will seldom yell. One time He did yell at me, but that was to tell me to get off the freeway just before my rear engine sports car exploded into flames, which is a story for a different time. So, yes, sometimes He does yell, but seldom. Most of the time, His voice is quiet, even a whisper that sounds calming, reassuring, encouraging. If we want to hear Him, we must train ourselves to be quiet. Shhh! Be quiet! Listen! Hear and trust the voice of a God that loves you and wants to heal your deepest cuts.

I would not be at all surprised that, after listening to His loving voice, you decide to develop a relationship with Him to secure ongoing health. Much of the time, after the cut has healed, a scar remains. God can turn ugly scars into sparkling facets that cast divine light in different patterns and sparkling colors. Those scars can even provide a platform from which we can help assure other cut ones that there is life and beauty if they, too, will simply trustingly listen to the Divine Glass Maker, a.k.a. Master Physician. What tormenting memory regularly visits you? What devastating pain will not allow you to live without fear or shame? What is the heartbreak that is preventing you from moving forward? Trust God. He's got this.

A fine crystal vase not only has a distinct appearance but also makes a clear sound when you flick it with your finger—a strong, satisfying ping. Crystal even makes music when you push your wet fingertip around the rim (think Sandra Bullock in *Miss Congeniality*). What sound do you make when someone flicks or pushes you? When someone has stretched your patience and tested your serenity? Your husband, maybe? "If he does that *one more time*." Your kids? "How *many times* do I have to tell you?" What sound? A few come to mind—cutting sarcasm, harsh accusations, and punishing corrections, just to name a few.

Some of us have gotten so used to our sound that we do not even recognize its crush. Comedian Bill Hicks jokes, "I don't mean to sound bitter, cold, or cruel, but I am, so that's how it comes out." The truth is that whatever that sound is on the inside, it will echo on the outside—somehow, somewhere. Are you grateful for all that life holds? Pleasant sound. Tired, overwhelmed, and stressed? Troubled sound. Afraid, sad, or frustrated? Angry sound. It is only as we allow God to change our internal, oh-so-private dialogue that our public dialogue will transform. I am not talking about fake sweetness—no Stepford females here. I am talking about a clear, strong, and heartwarming voice that has real potential to make a lasting impact in a culture of cutting, harsh, and punishing.

This demands lasting change, and that change can happen only from the inside out. Most often, it is not enough to want to change or even to decide to change. The change must happen in the heart, or it can't be maintained. This reminds me of a couple of closely related phrases that may be recognized by my Alcoholics Anonymous friends.

The first is "dry drunk," and the second is "white-knuckle sobriety." A dry drunk is someone who has quit drinking alcohol but has not made the internal changes needed to bring about changes in behavior. So a dry drunk is not drinking but still living life in the same destructive way. White-knuckle sobriety is using sheer willpower to stay sober. Again, not drinking, but living a miserable life of barely holding on. AA teaches that people with an alcohol addiction need to look to something greater than themselves to recover. That something is a *someone*—a Master Glass Maker. We are all, every one of us, trying to recover from something that has cut and damaged our souls. Our only hope is that Master Glass Maker, who is passionate about every piece He has created. As we learn to trust Him with every facet of our lives, our inner being will transform and, voilà! A work of art.

For your reflection:

- ➲ *Can you believe that there is a Master Creator who has designed you to be a true work of art?*
- ➲ *Will you trust God to use the "cuts of life" to make the best version of you?*
- ➲ *What is your sound when you have been "flicked"?*

It is art that makes life,
makes interest, makes importance and
I know of no substitute whatever for
the force and beauty of its process.

—Max Eastman

CHAPTER 3

RAKU POT

"This lump of clay has a mind of its own. It wants to stay a lump and not change. We, as the potter, must mold it and form it into the shape that we want it to be." Those were the first words from my teacher in my beginners pottery class, and while she thought she was talking about clay, I had the definite impression she was talking about my relationship with God. You may think that is a bit of a reach, but the Bible says: "Still, God, you are our Father. We're the clay and you're our potter: All of us are what you made us." Isaiah 64:8 (The Message).

There it is. Life is simpler and more fulfilling as we recognize that there is a Master Potter, and He has made us for a divine plan and purpose. It is one thing to make that statement but entirely another to ask ourselves this question: "How would I live if the certainty that I have been created for a divine plan and purpose guided my every moment, every decision, every relationship?"

After being birthed in Japan, raku pottery became Americanized during the mid-twentieth century. This organic art form is known for being simple and unpretentious. Raku is a many-step process, and each step must be fully completed before moving on. First, the raku artist carefully and intentionally shapes the clay by hand or on a wheel and must be careful that the clay is not too thick or too thin, that the walls and floor of the pot are of the same thickness. The artist then fires the piece in a kiln before placing it into a container with flammable materials such as newspaper, pine needles, or sawdust. The red-hot pot causes the material to flame, and then the container is completely covered with a lid to choke out the flame and create smoke. Smoking the pot gives it the unique raku look. The artist then "quenches" the pot by plunging it into cold water and quickly cooling it to stop the heat and oxidation process. A good scrubbing to remove carbon residue is the final step to presenting a gorgeous piece.

My raku pot friend is educated, well-traveled, and unique. She also gets frustrated when things do not happen as she thinks they should—and she almost always has an opinion of how they should. Stepping outside of her intellect and accepting things that she cannot understand is problematic. I can see her animated gestures as she continuously questions and debates, trying to let God be

God and yet trying to help life just make sense. Get ready, I am going to state some deep truth right now: Life often simply does not make sense! Author Tom Clancy said: "The difference between fiction and reality? Fiction has to make sense."

Yes, we use the good sense God gave us to think and reason, but there comes a moment in time that, by faith, we release control and agree to the full completion of the process that the Master Potter has planned. Or, as my husband tells me, "Stop trying to be the master of the universe." Trust me, the career of master of the universe can be very demanding and always exhausting. Sometimes the most difficult obstacle we must hurdle on our path to faith is the intellect.

The raku technique subjects the clay to constant extreme stress, increasing the risk of breakage. One wrong step, from construction to quenching, can cause breakage. A master raku potter knows the correct thickness of the clay, the exact temperature to fire, how long to smoke, and when to quench to create the most beautiful piece possible. Timing is crucial, and the raku pot must endure the process until fully completed. I have seen a fair share of raku pots that have had the bottoms blown out due to a flawed process. *Endurance* is our ability or strength to continue despite adverse conditions and presents an interesting paradox. While life itself demands that we continue, we detest adverse conditions. But it is those very adverse conditions that produce the endurance that we need to continue! Endurance is created only in trouble, distress, or pressure—think baby chick struggling to emerge from the egg. Lack of suffering results in comparative uselessness.

Byron Janis is a brilliant and critically acclaimed concert pianist and composer. He is considered one of the great pianists of the twentieth century. He made his Carnegie Hall debut at age twenty. At age forty-five, he noticed a red patch on his finger that was accompanied by a great deal of pain. Soon afterward, he was diagnosed with excruciating psoriatic arthritis in both hands and wrists, causing swollen joints and bone damage. Now, this diagnosis would have been devastating for anyone, but what do you do if your livelihood and your passion depend on your hands? If you are Byron Janis, you relieve some of the pain with medications, adjust your technique, and keep playing. In fact, he kept the illness a secret for twelve years, telling no one except his wife and a few close friends. Later on, some of the bones of his fingers fused together, and still he refused to give up. He had several surgeries and tried every possible solution, and he endured.

"It was a life-and-death struggle for me every day for years," Janis said. "At every point I thought of not being able to continue performing, and it terrified me. Music, after all, was my life, my world, my passion." In 1985 Byron Janis became a spokesman for the Arthritis Foundation, and in 2014, he celebrated his eighty-sixth birthday by playing a Chopin waltz at a reception in Chicago. He is convinced that constantly using his fingers despite the pain has kept him from having totally deformed hands.

We will not all be concert pianists, although I did take accordion lessons some years ago and got rather good at playing "The Beer Barrel Polka." No, we will not all be concert pianists, but everyone faces seemingly impossible circumstances and can be tempted to quit, to give up before we see the beauty in the completion of the process. Do not give up! Press on and press through! Stopping the process too soon, or quenching before the pot is fully smoked, before the Master's plan is fully accomplished, does not allow for the full beauty of the piece to be realized.

My raku pot friend requires life to happen quickly, with fast resolutions to problems. But that quick way of life is exhausting. Most of us live it. Schedules and calendars and meetings, oh my! There is no small amount of conviction in Stephen Covey's words: "People expect us to be busy, overworked. It's become a status symbol in our society—if we're busy, we're important; if we're not busy, we're almost embarrassed to admit it."

Busyness is where we get our security. It's validating, popular, and pleasing. It's also a good excuse for not dealing with the first things in our lives. "I'd love to spend quality time with you, but I have to work. There's this deadline. It's urgent. Of course, you understand." "I just don't have time to exercise. I know it's important, but there are so many pressing things right now. Maybe when things slow down a little." We hide behind the shield of busy, holding at a distance essential interaction, interaction that might be challenging or uncomfortable but also just might be the key to significant personal growth and fulfillment. And the stress of our busyness can lead to many diseases. Asthma, diabetes, headaches, heart disease, depression—all can be linked to stress.

Our lives are a work in progress, and, just like a raku pot, if that process is too speedy, there is a better than fair chance that we will be weak and risk breakage. In my beginners pottery class, as my teacher was demonstrating throwing a pot on the wheel, we could see a strange stripe appear in the clay, indicating a weak area. She said, "The clay is exhausted." Yes, she used the word *exhausted.* "We have to set it aside to rest." She assured us that after allowing it to rest, the clay could be reclaimed and rescued, meaning that setting aside the clay would give it new life and the potter could then work with it. If you feel exhausted and stressed, the Master Potter may have to set you aside for a time so that you can be rescued and given new life.

One aspect of raku work that makes it uncertain is that you simply never know what you are going to get until the entire process is completed. Each stress-filled step changes the look of the finished piece. What starts as an average clay pot just may end up being a beautiful and rare raku pot.

My precious mother was an excellent wife and mother, the picture of sweet grace, an unpretentious woman. Everyone was always welcome at her table for food and laughter. Mom did love to laugh. Her early life was complicated by never knowing the love of her abusive father. She did not consider herself an excellent anything, often struggling with a sense of inadequacy. But she was a woman who knew and trusted the Master Potter. She taught her children great love, but it was not until the end of her life, as hundreds of people came to express their love and respect for her, that it became clear this unassuming clay pot was a piece of beautiful and rare raku. Mom loved God, loved her family, and quietly allowed the completion of the Master Potter's process for her life. I invite you to allow the full completion of God's full plan and purpose for your life. You will never know your true beauty until the process is complete.

For your reflection:

- *Can you resign as master of the universe and let God be God?*
- *What is your connection to busyness?*
- *Are you exhausted or stressed? Will you allow God to set you aside for a time so that you can be rescued?*
- *Will you agree to press on to see through to completion God's plan for your life?*

I'm a Little Teapot

I'm a little teapot
Short and stout.
Here is my handle,
Here is my spout.

When I get all steamed up
Hear me shout:
"Tip me over
and pour me out!"

—American Children's Song, 1939

CHAPTER 4

BRIGHTLY COLORED TEAPOT

"But I do not *want* to be a teapot!" I thought to myself in a whiny, hands-on-the-hips sort of way. That was one of my first thoughts when I realized that this was the pot that had been chosen for me. No, I do not want to be a teapot. Teapots are everywhere. Nearly every home has a teapot, and they are simply too ordinary. You know—average. The fact that it was a brightly colored teapot made little difference. Still average. People *like* teapots, but they do not necessarily *admire* teapots. Teapots are not typically revered for their artistic rarity. Teapots, brightly colored or not, are basically utilitarian. I want to be a tall and lovely cut crystal vase or an exotic raku pot—anything but a regular, everyday teapot. And then there is that whole "short and stout" thing. It seemed to me that I was a lesser vessel than the cut crystal vase or the raku pot.

And so began the comparison. We probably all have heard much about the danger of comparing ourselves to others. Google it and you will find articles, blogs, and sermons about how comparing ourselves to others can hinder and hurt us. I want to go on record as saying that making comparisons is not a bad thing. *To compare* simply means to evaluate, to notice resemblances or differences. To stop making comparisons, we would have to remove part of our cerebral cortex. Comparing is part of our design. We often compare ourselves with someone we admire to emulate them. We are looking to someone who has gone before us to learn from their lives. Comparison can inspire us to improve. Even the Apostle Paul said, "Follow my example as I follow the example of Christ." 1 Corinthians 11:1. That cannot be accomplished without comparison.

No, comparison itself is not unhealthy. It is what we do with that comparison that can be so very damaging. As we struggle to acknowledge and accept our differences, or our similarities, we will gravitate toward value judgments. A value judgment is deciding that something or someone is good or bad, right or wrong, useful or not, based on comparison. When comparing ourselves to other people leads to a value judgment, there is a very real possibility that we have taken that comparison to a dangerous place. We often use elementary words like *good* or *bad*, *right* or *wrong*, *pretty* or *ugly*, *smart* or *dumb* to describe our own worth based on how we stack up against others—physically, intellectually, financially, relationally, and even spiritually. Once that judgment is made, there are only two places we can go—superiority or inferiority. Neither of these is acceptable, and feeling superior or inferior often leads to detrimental decisions.

It has been said, "Everybody is a genius. But if you judge a fish by its ability to climb a tree, it will live its whole life believing that it is stupid." Some of us rainbow trout have spent way too much time trying to climb that oak, and we cannot make any headway! The time has come for us to accept our troutness and swim, swim, swim for all we are worth. Only then will we realize our potential to be the strongest, fastest, most beautiful fish we can be.

It's easy to find lists of the dangers of comparing ourselves to others, but I cannot help but wonder, why do we do it? Why is the comparison path so natural for us? Why does it seem almost second nature? To figure it out, let us go back to the beginning, the book of beginnings. We all know the story of Adam and Eve in the garden. God tells Adam that he can eat the fruit of *any tree* in the garden except the tree of knowledge of good and evil. One day Eve is hanging around the garden and hears the voice of the tempter (more than a few of us have heard that voice), and that is where the trouble begins.

The serpent was clever, more clever than any wild animal God had made. He spoke to the Woman: "Do I understand that God told you not to eat from any tree in the garden?"

The Woman said to the serpent, "Not at all. We can eat from the trees in the garden. It's only about the tree in the middle of the garden that God said, 'Don't eat from it; don't even touch it or you'll die.'"

The serpent told the Woman, "You won't die. God knows that the moment you eat from that tree, you'll see what's really going on. You'll be just like God, knowing everything, ranging all the way from good to evil."

When the Woman saw that the tree looked like good eating and realized what she would get out of it—she'd know everything!—she took and ate the fruit and then gave some to her husband, and he ate." Genesis 3:1-6 (The Message).

Do you see it? Eve looked and saw that the tree would be "good." There it is, right there: The only way that the fruit could be "good" was in comparison to other fruit. She made a comparison and a value judgment, which then led her to the mother of all detrimental decisions, severely impacting the generations to come. Could this be why comparing comes so easily for most of us? Remember that comparison itself is not unhealthy; the catch comes in deciding exactly what to do with that comparison, and that is a soul issue. Eve was told she could eat the *fruit of any tree* in the garden except the fruit of the tree of knowledge of good and evil. *Any fruit but one.* Lo and behold, Eve wanted that one fruit from that one tree, and she was not going to be content until she took and ate it.

Eve wanted that fruit, and I wanted to be a different vessel. Both of us had contentment problems. *Contentment* is the state of being happy and satisfied or feeling free from worry or restlessness. May I please see a show of hands of those people who are right now, in this moment, fully content? OK. Now may I please see a show of hands of those who have become so used to discontent that you don't even recognize it?

Recently I was reading a book that suggested a list of attitudes and behaviors that we need to look at for our personal growth. This list included issues such as anxiety, bossiness, and stubbornness—all of which I may or may not have a problem with. As I worked my way down the list, the word *covetousness* showed up. I put a question mark next to the word and moved on. I was not exactly sure what covetousness was, but it certainly was not one of my concerns! After all, it was one of the Ten Commandments, and I was all good with those, right? The trouble was that the word would not go away. It stuck to me. It roamed around in my head and incessantly showed up in books and articles and conversations. Finally, I figured out that maybe, just maybe, I should pay attention.

Covetousness is the strong desire to have that which belongs to someone else and is closely related to *envy*. Defensively, I thought, "Not my issue! I don't really want someone else's house or car or career or husband." Finally, this thought came to me: "Covetousness reflects discontentment," and discontentment is an old familiar acquaintance of mine.

To look at our contentment, or our lack of contentment, requires us to take a deep dive into the very core of our soul, and it often does not have much to do with houses, cars or careers or husbands. *Cool Runnings* is one of my all-time favorite movies and has one of my favorite movie lines. If you have not seen this movie, you absolutely should watch it. John Candy's character was a victorious Olympic bobsledder. After winning two gold medals, he cheated in the 1972 Winter Olympics competition and had his medals stripped. He ended up coaching the Jamaican bobsled team for the 1988 Winter Olympics. The captain of this team asked him why he cheated. He explained that he had to keep winning and followed up with: "A gold medal is a wonderful thing. But if you're not enough without it, you'll never be enough with it."

Let that settle for a minute. How often do we chase people, possessions, or accolades because, ultimately, we are deeply afraid that we are simply not enough without them? For me, the true core of covetousness, and thereby discontentment, was not that I wanted what someone else *owned*, I wanted to *be* someone else because I could never be enough. That, my friends, is some deep envy.

If the need to make comparisons that lead to envy and threaten our soul peace is so deep in our human DNA, how do we destroy the threat? How do we break this exhausting mindset and walk a path to freedom? The first step on this path is to acknowledge the threat. We cannot heal what we do not acknowledge, and there is no shame in truth-telling. Shame hides in darkness, and its power dissipates in light. Look honestly at this threat and call it what it is.

Next, bring the truth to God. Ask Him what is behind the envy. Do you struggle to feel good enough? Do you believe that person who said, "You'll never amount to much"? Were you called names as a kid? Abused? Come from great family dysfunction? There are so many hindrances that can sabotage our soul health. I can safely say that not one of us had the perfect earthly father. Not one. It is OK to say that out loud. Come on! Join the club! Not one of us had the perfect earthly father, but you do have a Divine Father, a Good Father, who cares for and protects His children and who genuinely wants you to be free from those ideas, mindsets, and behaviors that damage your soul.

Behaviors consistently practiced lead to habits. Applying these next two habits with conviction and intentionality can dismantle the power of envy. First, grasp after and obtain gratefulness. We have heard this so often, but that cannot lessen its importance. Gratefulness lifts our feelings. Are you depressed, oppressed, just generally feeling down? Begin right now to express gratitude—for everything and anything. It does not matter how seemingly small or large, important or unimportant. Just begin to say, "I am thankful for . . ." and see if you do not experience your feelings beginning to lift. Gratefulness is a habit that you can cultivate and grow. I'm not naturally a grateful person. I look through lenses that tend to see what needs improvement, but I am working on developing the gratitude habit. It's helpful to write down what you are feeling grateful for and even to keep a gratefulness journal. At first, it may seem awkward, but start small and keep going. In time, you will discover that gratefulness overpowers envy.

The second behavior that dismantles envy is to celebrate other people. Think about the last time you saw a social media post or got a text or phone call that reported someone else's good news. Were you able to immediately celebrate that good news as if you owned it, or did you feel just the slightest tinge of resentment? Did the comparisons multiply before you could prevent them? You can triumph over this resentment by applauding—figuratively and literally. Just the physical act of clapping for other people redirects our thoughts and has the potential to crush resentment and envy. Wouldn't it be funny if we just spontaneously broke into applause in public celebration of others? Yes, perhaps a bit unexpected and crazy, but definitely funny. This may seem like an oversimplification, but we have the power to expose and demolish thoughts, behaviors, and habits that threaten our peace. We are always one decision away from a completely different life.

The teapot in our story is specifically a "brightly colored teapot." I am drawn to bright clothing, jewelry, and décor. My sisters made fun of me the one time that I decided to wear gold lamé shoes—I promise I only did it one time! Still, I like bright. A teapot lesson for me is that I can be as bright as I want to be, but my primary purpose is utilitarian. It is my job to pour out God's grace and mercy on anyone who will listen, and I have found that helping people understand the overwhelming truth of God's love is my absolute favorite endeavor. After many years of living as a brightly colored teapot, I can finally admit that I like this assignment. I still do not want to be "short and stout," but I love being a vessel used to bring light, life, and love.

We are *not* who other people say we are. We are *not* even who we say we are. We are *only* who the Creator designed us to be. Communicating openly and honestly with the Creator God, who is Love (not simply loving, but *IS* Love), can direct us to the truth of exactly who we are created to be. However, some view God as restrictive, arbitrary, judgmental, critical, and disapproving. This simply could not be further from the truth. God's audacious plan invites us to live boldly and fearlessly—fully engaged with people and circumstances. He welcomes us to thrive, not simply survive. He also knows that engaging in specific behaviors can shatter us, and His Love demands restrictions needed for our health and safety. Repeat after me: "God is God, and I am not." His love is fully complete, unconditional, and never-ending.

It has taken many years and many miles to realize that I am divinely and wonderfully designed. With all my faults and frailties, I must choose to continually and intentionally believe that God has rescued me from hindrances. I am created for a purpose, and that purpose matters. A friend recently told me that the teapot is central to gatherings at her home. People relax and sigh a breath of release with a cup of tea in their hands, and it is the teapot that pours that warmth and love. It is God's Grace that empowers us to dismantle ruthless beliefs that so easily chip away at our heart and persuade us that we are less. Only in giving place to that Grace, do we have any hope of living a full and contented life. Kids are asked, "What do you want to be when you grow up?" A ballerina, astronaut, police officer, movie star—so many choices. What a difference it would make if we passionately taught ourselves and our children to first answer that question with a one-word answer: "Me!"

*"To be yourself in a world that is
constantly trying to make you
something else is the greatest accomplishment."*
—Ralph Waldo Emerson

For your reflection:

- ➲ *How do you handle comparison? Does it encourage you to better things? Does it provoke envy?*
- ➲ *Are you generally content? Why or why not?*
- ➲ *What do you have to be grateful for?*
- ➲ *Who can you celebrate?*
- ➲ *Can you accept God's invitation to a bold and thriving life?*

We are all wounded. But wounds are necessary for his healing light to enter into our beings. Without wounds and failure and frustrations and defeats, there will be no opening for his brilliance to trickle in and invade our lives. Failures in life are courses with very high tuition fees, so I don't cut classes and miss my lessons: on humility, on patience, on hope, on asking others for help, on listening to God, on trying again and again and again.

—Bo Sanchez

CHAPTER 5

MOSAIC POT

Eventually, another vessel was added to our happy little fellowship. I was at a women's event telling them about our collection of pots when, at the last minute, I decided to throw in a mosaic pot that I happened to have. As I began to talk, a lovely young lady in the audience hid her face in her hands and began to cry uncontrollably. Being the astute woman that I am, I knew immediately that something important was happening, and it had something to do with mosaics.

A mosaic is a pattern or image crafted with small pieces of colored stone, glass, or ceramic held in place by plaster or mortar. The name Mosaic means "Pattern of Pieces." So a mosaic is made of broken pieces. Often these pieces start life as something whole but are broken in life's process. Instead of just tossing away the broken bits, the mosaic artist carefully rescues each piece and painstakingly places each one in a pattern to create something brand-new and strikingly beautiful. The artist must carefully think out the placement of each piece so that they all correspond and create a cohesive art piece. This new version is one of a kind—no two mosaics are the same. My pot is made of royal blue mirror glass pieces with small bits of fragmented china separating the mirrors. There has never been and never will be another exactly like it.

Curiously, brokenness can be either beneficial or devastating. An example of beneficial brokenness is the germinating seed that breaks to allow the roots to establish, or the baby bird that gains strength to emerge from the egg by having to break the shell. Brokenness is completely devastating only when all hope is gone that wholeness can ever be rescued or restored. Hope is anticipation and an expectation that good is on the way. It is crucial to explicitly determine what anchor our hope is chained to. Reason demands that that anchor be rock steady, unlike any person, situation, bank account, or even hope itself. What is your hope fastened to?

Many years ago, my husband and I had a business, and through some crazy circumstances, some caused by us and some not caused by us, we were forced to sell to a larger company. When the considerable dust settled, we were left with scarcely enough to buy groceries. Excruciating, agonizing, terrible—go ahead, insert your own word here for "thought I was going to die." Fortunately, our pastor told my crumpled-on-the-floor husband that he was excited for us because we were now positioned to see God's miracles firsthand. Really? Did I mention my husband was crumpled on the floor? That pastor's words caused us to attach our hope to God in unfamiliar and untried ways.

Day after day, money enough appeared to sustain us—money from family, a refund check, a rebate. Never large amounts, just enough to get us through. As time passed, we even grew comfortable strapping all hope to God, the only conceivable steady and trustworthy anchor. Learning gigantic lessons about faith and hope, we were slightly melancholy when we emerged from this stint. Hope is the marvel that gives us the ability to face the future, trusting that better is coming. Brokenness is final only when all hope is lost.

Remember the young lady in the audience? What I did not know until later was that she believed that she was irretrievably broken. She had made some seriously damaging life choices, and she was suffering the consequences of those choices. Having lost hope, she showed up at this event only because her mother wanted her to be there. Fortunately, the Expert Mosaic Artist knew she was coming and orchestrated a message for her. He will rescue the broken shards of your soul and create an entirely original vessel that can have purpose beyond your wildest imagination. You can trust me because I know this to be true. If you spend enough time with me and look very carefully, you can just barely see the mortar holding the broken pieces in place.

As a child, it never seemed like I "fit." I suspect that I was a challenging and weird kid. My parents did not quite know what to do with me. I was a good student, but being profoundly shy and reticent made social situations torturous. For about a minute and a half, I thought I had found a place in our little Pentecostal church, but even that did not last. It seemed like other people belonged and had their place, but not me. Two weeks after my eighteenth birthday, I left my solid Midwestern home and family and fled to California, throwing off all restraint. I was desperate to find my place, desperate to know that my existence mattered, and desperate to know deep love.

I did not have a plan. What I had was an empty place in my soul that required filling, so I did anything and everything that seemed good to me, and *good* was defined as anything unfamiliar, thrilling, and entertaining. After thirteen years of "good," I was miserable, drained, and empty—spirit, soul, and body. I was so extremely weary. Thick darkness surrounded me, and I had become accustomed to chaos. Peace was out of the question.

One morning I was in my kitchen cleaning up after a night-before party, and I heard a man talking in my living room. Now, this might not seem strange except for the fact that I was the only one home. With dish cloth in hand, suds dripping, I dashed into the living room. A man was definitely there, and he was definitely talking. And he was speaking directly to me. It's just that he was on the television. I know, it sounds bizarre, and I cannot tell you how I knew that he was targeting me. I just knew. With wide-eyed understanding, I stared at him, and this is what he said: "Haven't you run long enough? Jesus is standing right there. If you will put your hand in His, He will lead you into all peace." Recognizing this as a divine moment (I told you I was astute), I simply whispered, "OK." At that very instant, I saw Jesus. I will say that again. I saw Jesus. I do not know if I saw Him as a spiritual picture or if He was standing with me, but I saw Him.

Thirty-five years after this astonishing experience, I still hold in my mind the remarkably vivid image of His eyes as we gazed at each other. In the eyes of Jesus are deep, deep pools of love. Many bottomless pools filled with immeasurable love. I realized that Jesus fully loved me. He saw the truth of my chaos-filled life and fully loved this addicted party girl whose marriage was on the brink of failure. This was love like no other. Unique and absolute.

For the first time in my life, I knew where I belonged. I tumbled into those pools of love and have not looked back. At that whispered "OK," the Divine Mosaic Artist rescued the first broken fragment and tenderly positioned it on this brand-new vessel. The first mosaic piece was placed, and, to this day, He continues to rescue my broken pieces. This process won't be completed this side of heaven, but from one mosaic to another, God delights to restore our shattered soul. We simply must give Him the "OK," whispered or shouted. The Expert Mosaic Artist is waiting for us to give Him permission to rescue us.

For your reflection:

- *Do you ever wonder if you are too far gone? Have you made too many mistakes, too many bad choices?*
- *Do you dare to believe that Jesus has the same love for you that He has for me?*
- *Will you trust the Divine Mosaic Artist with your broken bits and allow Him to make someone brand-new?*

We very often prayed that God would make us vessels to be filled with divine presence, fit for His use, whatever He had planned for us. We even prayed that He would break us of our selfishness and pride so that we could be divinely used.

CHAPTER 6

THE BREAKDOWN

Our little fellowship of pots was astonished by the lessons that the Master Potter had for us, but the most acute lesson was still to come. Running random errands one day, I came across and purchased perfect versions of each of the pots. Within one six-hour period, I held in my hands exquisite pieces of glassware—one cut crystal vase, one raku pot, and one brightly colored teapot. At our next meeting, bursting with anticipation, I laughed as I presented the ladies with each carefully wrapped piece. Think little kid at Christmas. It seemed so surreal that God—*the* God, the Creator of the Universe—would speak to us in this way and cherry-pick an appropriate vessel fit exclusively for each of us.

We each took our pot and chose a visible place of honor in our homes to display our prized treasure. We pointed them out to visitors and happily explained our grand pot adventure. We were so honored and felt oh so special—for about a month. Four weeks after the pots took their respective places, I again heard the very same voice that told us exactly which vessels we were. However, the message was vastly different this time. I heard these words: "Break the pots." The words were crystal clear, but I sat still, silently still, hoping that maybe, just maybe, they were not so clear. Again, "Break the pots."

Teary-eyed, I hesitantly began explaining to the ladies what I had heard. Crystal Vase and Raku Pot stared at me as I calmly stated, "We have to break the pots." Silent disbelief for a few minutes. You have heard it said, "Be careful what you pray for." Morgan Freeman as God in the movie *Evan Almighty*, said this: "Let me ask you something. If someone prays for patience, you think God gives them patience? Or does he give them the opportunity to be patient? If he prayed for courage, does God give him courage, or does he give him opportunities to be courageous? If someone prayed for the family to be closer, do you think God zaps them with warm, fuzzy feelings, or does he give them opportunities to love each other?" Much of the time, we would choose zapping, but most of the time, that is not how divine business is conducted.

The directive to break the pots took more than a few minutes to sink in, and although we had prayed many times that God would break us of our selfishness and pride so that we could be divinely used, well, look at these distinct responses:

Beautiful Cut Crystal Vase laughed through tears. Because God had walked with her through such challenging life circumstances, she fully recognized that she could trust Him no matter what came down the pike. She was so secure in His complete love for her that she could laugh at the future.

Do you dare look at the future and laugh? For many of us, our future is fear-filled, and rightly so. Our world can be painful and outrageously unsafe, and we have experienced its aching sorrow. Please know that there is a Divine Glass Maker who will rescue your suffering and create a lovely vessel usable for a purpose that is beyond your wildest imagination.

Exotic Raku Pot emphatically folded her arms and declared, "Absolutely not! That is ridiculous! I love my beautiful pot, and I am not breaking it! What a waste of money!" Smashing the pot made no sense to her, so she was quick to write it off as nonsense. It took her a bit of time to get to the understanding that there is God's path and our path, and these two paths very often go in different directions. Here is the question that you and I absolutely must answer. I do not believe that I cannot overstate the importance of answering this one question: "Do I choose to live this one life that I have been given according to my finite understanding or according to the infinite love, guidance, and care of a Good Father who just happens to be the Creator of all things?"

I can hear you: "Well, if you're going to put it *that* way." The response to this question can be the beginning of a brand-new life, a fresh life filled with hope and peace. Raku Pot eventually came around and agreed to break her pot, but even then, she did it her way, grinding it into tiny pieces. I think that made God shake His head a bit and smile.

Brightly Colored Teapot approached the breaking with tears. She understood that God was asking her to yield the selfishness, pride, and control that held way more influence in her life than she wanted them to, and yielding was a frightening proposition. Unsure of her identity without them, she also understood that if she was going to see progress to soul health, she was going to have to let go of the rigid grip that they had on her life, and breaking was going to have to happen.

I have firsthand knowledge that Teapot took the teapot, wrapped it in a plastic bag (she was smart enough to know that if she made a mess, she would have to clean it up), stood on a chair, and hurled it onto the concrete patio. Remarkably, the instant the teapot hit the concrete and broke into many pieces, something significant also broke in my soul. Experiencing an overwhelming freedom of release, I sat down on the concrete, put my hands over my face, and ugly cried, really not caring who saw ugly. I was forever different, not perfect, but different. I had a strong willingness to walk with the Master Potter and allow Him to direct my future, knowing that even in breaking, I can trust this Good, Good Father, who cares for and protects His children.

Just in case you are wondering what kind of vessel you are, let me give a word of guidance. I hope that you noticed in our little gathering of pots that we did not choose our vessel—God chose. With sensitive care, the Divine Glass Maker/Master Potter/Divine Mosaic Artist chose, knowing exactly the lessons that would benefit. While God is superior in every way, He is also very personal. He sees the truth of your present reality, and He has chosen you as a vessel to hold His magnificent presence. Allow Him to define you. If I am a vessel to be filled and used for divine purpose, then so are you. If God can take my averageness (that really is a word) and make it divine, then He will do the same for you. You can become a holder of the Divine. Go ahead. Pry your fingers off the vessel that is your life and let Him define your worth. He thinks you are fabulous.

For your reflection:

Can you dare to believe that God's plan, through Jesus, will relieve your fears, flaws, and failures and guide you to the Divine?

Why do I need to be rescued?

∞

We are all born with sin, and we all personally choose to sin. Sin is what separates us from God. Sin is what has us on the path to eternal destruction.

How can I be rescued? Rescued from what?

∞

Because of our sin, we all deserve death. While the physical consequence of sin is physical death, that is not the only kind of death that results from sin. All sin is ultimately committed against an eternal and infinite God. Because of that, the just penalty for our sin is also eternal and infinite. What we need to be rescued from is eternal destruction.

How does God rescue?

∽

Because the just penalty for sin is infinite and eternal, only God could pay the penalty, because only He is infinite and eternal. But God, in His divine nature, could not die.

So God became a human being in the person of Jesus Christ. He willingly sacrificed Himself for us, allowing Himself to be crucified. Jesus's death on the cross was the perfect and complete payment for our sin. He took the consequences we deserved. Jesus's resurrection from the dead demonstrated that His death was indeed the perfect sacrifice for sin.

How can I be rescued?

∽

God has already done all the work. All you must do is receive, in faith, the salvation God offers. Fully trust in Jesus alone as the payment for your sins.